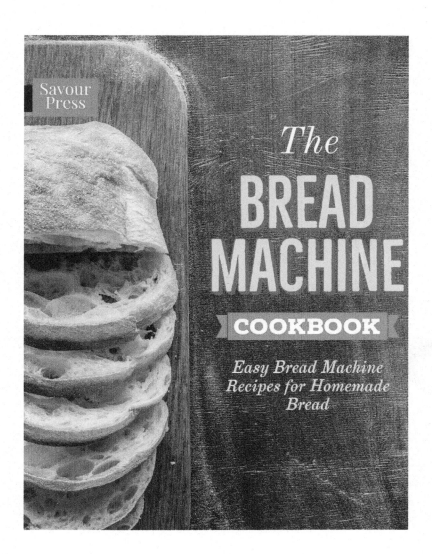

Savour Press

The

BREAD MACHINE

COOKBOOK

Easy Bread Machine Recipes for Homemade Bread

BREAD MACHINE RECIPES

EASY AND NUTRITIOUS BREAD MACHINE RECIPES

By
Savour Press
Copyright © by Wentworth Publishing House

Published by
Savour Press, a DBA of Wentworth Publishing House

Let's get it started!

Welcome to Savour. Today, our daily chores have become so easy with all the modern home and kitchen gadgets available. There are no more alibis, why you can't do them quickly and with precision. When it comes to preparing the best breads in the world, there is nothing impossible if you look for ways that will make them much easier. Among the things that you might consider is to use a bread machine pan or bread maker to lessen your time in preparing the ingredients, such as, whisking, kneading, rolling, blending, sifting, caramelizing, sieving, and to name a few. By clicking the bread machine, your bread will be ready in two to three hours, or some bread types could take up in less than an hour. Our thrust is to teach you the basics of baking using the bread maker, so as not to deprive you and your loved ones with the best breads ever made. We firmly believe that baking can be made by everyone; even kids could do it, and why can't you?

About This Book

Is baking possible by someone who has no background about this cooking method? This is a common question we encounter by some people who don't believe in their capabilities. *Savour* thinks differently. We believe that you can be someone who is adept in the kitchen, if you entrust to us everything that you want to know. With our 45 best bread machine recipes, we know outright that you can be the best baker in your family. Our cookbook comprises different bread types, such as twists, loafs, breads, naan, focaccia, johns, flatbread, buns, bagels, crescents, Kolaches, breadsticks, Panettone and a lot more. You will notice that breads have a lot of recipes, and once you have mastered the use of bread machine pan, you can give them a twist, or incorporate the methods to come up with another bread type, like for example, you will use the basic bread recipe to make them into loaf bread. Let's get ready to have a fun time!

CONTENTS

INTRODUCTION

Breads are one of the oldest types of foods that have been known thousands of years ago. In fact, breads were already prepared in biblical times. Its versatility will never have an end. So here, *Savour* introduces you the art of making bread with the use of bread machine pan. The basic thing that you must do is to put all ingredients in their order of appearance based on the manual suggestion. Usually, it starts with warm water or warm milk, and followed by other ingredients and finally ending up with active dry yeast. After putting the ingredients in the machine, you will be asked to select the dough or bread setting, and then check the dough after 5 minutes of mixing, choose crust color, loaf size, and you will be asked to add a tablespoon of water or flour if needed and then remove the dough, and the other instructions follow depending on the type of bread that you will be preparing. You will find in this edition our 45 bread machine recipes, and some of them are contest winners in their respective bread types.

Enjoy!

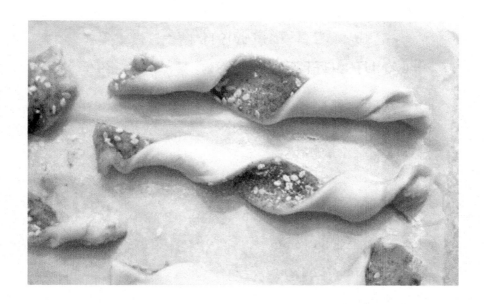

TWISTS

PEANUT BUTTER TWISTS

These contest winning twists will change your impression on breads. The twists are packed with creamy peanut butter and butter filling and topped with creamy peanut butter icing. The soft inside of the twists are creamylicious, which is a perfect breakfast treat.

Servings: 2 dozens

Ingredients

3/4 cup **(70° to 80°) water**

1/3 cup softened **butter**

1 large **egg**

1/4 cup of **nonfat dry milk powder**

1/3 cup **sugar**

3/4 teaspoon **salt**

3 cups **bread flour**

2 1/4 teaspoons **active dry yeast**

For the filling:

1/4 cup softened **butter**

3/4 cup **creamy peanut butter**

1/3 cup **confectioners' sugar**

For the icing:

2 tablespoons **creamy peanut butter**

1 1/2 cups **confectioners' sugar**

5 to 7 tablespoons **warm water**

Directions

In a bread machine, put all eight ingredients

Press the dough setting, checking the dough after mixing for five minutes, and adding one to two tablespoons water or flour if necessary.

Place the dough on a surface dusted with flour, punch down and cover. Let stand for ten minutes.

Combine in a medium-bowl the filling ingredients. After ten minutes, roll the dough into a 24"by 8" rectangle.

Spread the filling on top within one-half inch of the edges. Fold the rectangle in half lengthwise, and cut into 24 pieces widthwise. Pinch the seams to seal and twist each thrice.

Arrange the dough on the greased baking sheets, about two inches apart.

Bake for fifteen to twenty minutes at 350 degrees Fahrenheit until nicely golden brown. Remove twist from the pans and let cool on wire racks.

Prepare the glaze by mixing in a bowl the peanut butter, confectioner's sugar and enough water; drizzle on the twists.

Note: The time-delay feature of the bread machine is not recommended to use for this recipe.

Serve!

Nutritional Information: 199 calories; 9 g fat (4 g saturated fat); 21 mg cholesterol; 172 mg sodium; 26 g carbohydrate; 13 g total sugars; 1 g dietary fiber; 5 g protein.

BREAD
HOLIDAY SWEET POTATO BREAD

This nutritious bread could be the one you are looking for when the weather is bad. With a cup of brewed coffee, munching this tasty bread, will give you comfort when you can't bear the cold season. Its chewy texture from marshmallows helps distract you from total discomfort.

Servings: 1 loaf (about 1-1/2 pounds)

Ingredients

1/2 cup plus 2 tablespoons **warm (70° to 80°) milk**

1 1/2 teaspoons **salt**

1 **lightly beaten egg**

2 tablespoons **brown sugar**

4 1/2 teaspoons **butter**

1/3 cup **miniature marshmallows**

3 cups **bread flour**

1/2 cup chopped canned drained **sweet potatoes**

2 1/2 teaspoons **active dry yeast**

Directions

Put together in a bread machine pan all bread ingredients in proper sequence as directed by the manufacturer.

Choose the basic bread setting, and then the crust color and loaf size, if it is available.

Start baking based on the machine instructions, making sure to check the dough after mixing for five minutes.

Add one to two tablespoons water or flour if necessary.

Serve!

Nutritional Information: 113 calories; 2 g fat (1 g saturated fat); 17 mg cholesterol; 245 mg sodium; 21 g carbohydrate; 4 g total sugars; 1 g dietary fiber; 4 g protein.

TRIPLE APPLE BREAD

What can you expect in apple bread flavored with applesauce, apple juice, butter and cinnamon aside from chopped apples? The bread is a winner when it comes to its flavor, tastes and texture. It is not so sweet, so you can eat more if you are watching your diet.

Servings: 1 loaf

Ingredients

3/4 cup finely chopped & peeled **apples**

1/4 cup **warm applesauce (70°-80°)**

3/4 cup **warm apple juice (70°-80°)**

1 teaspoon **ground cinnamon**

1 tablespoon **butter**

1 1/2 teaspoons **salt**

2 tablespoons **brown sugar**

2 cups **bread flour**

1/8 teaspoon **ground nutmeg**

2 1/2 teaspoons **active dry yeast**

1 cup **whole wheat flour**

Directions

In a bread machine pan, put all ingredients in sequence as suggested by the brand's manufacturer.

Choose basic bread setting, and chose crust and loaf size.

Bake the bread according to the manual instructions and inspect the dough after mixing is over.

Add in 1 to 2 tablespoons flour or dough to the machine.

Serve!

Nutritional Information: 101 calories; 1 g fat (0 g saturated fat); 2 mg cholesterol; 230 mg sodium; 21 g carbohydrate; 4 g total sugars; 2 g dietary fiber; 3 g protein.

RAISIN WHEAT BREAD

This wheat bread has a little of everything. It is a little crunchy, a little sweet, hearty, dense, and moist. The secret is the blend of molasses, honey, sunflower kernels, and raisins, olive oil with bread and wheat flours.

Servings: 1 loaf (16 slices)

Ingredients

1 1/4 cups plus 1 tablespoon **(70° to 80°) water**

2 tablespoons **honey**

2 tablespoons **olive oil**

1 1/2 teaspoon **salt**

2 tablespoons **molasses**

2/3 cup **raisins**

1/3 cup **unsalted sunflower kernels**

2 1/2 teaspoon **active dry yeast**

1 1/3 cups **bread flour**

2 cups **whole wheat flour**

Directions

Place in a bread machine pan the water, olive oil, honey, molasses, salt, sunflower kernels, raisins, whole wheat flour, bread flour, and yeast.

Read the manual when baking and check the dough when mixing is done after five minutes, adding one to two tablespoons of flour or water if necessary.

Just in case there is no wheat setting on your bread machine, use the basic setting directions instead.

Enjoy!

Nutritional Information: 164 calories; 4 g fat (0 g saturated fat); 0 mg cholesterol; 223 mg sodium; 29 g carbohydrate; 0 g total sugars; 3 g dietary fiber; 5 g protein.

ITALIAN SWEET BREAD

This smooth looking bread gives you a balanced sweetness and saltiness. This is the result of brushing the top of bread with egg wash and drizzling with Italian seasoning before putting in the oven. It is soft on the inside with the blend of egg and butter while the outside is golden brown.

Servings: 2 loaves (16 slices each)

Ingredients

1 cup warm **(70° to 80°) 2% milk**

1 lightly beaten large **egg**

1/4 cup **sugar**

2 tablespoons softened **butter**

2 teaspoons **active dry yeast**

3 cups **all-purpose flour**

1 teaspoon **salt**

Egg wash:

1 tablespoon **water**

1 large **egg**

Italian seasoning (optional)

Directions

Place all ingredients except for the egg wash in a bread machine pan in this order, milk, egg, butter, sugar, salt, flour and yeast.

Choose the dough setting and check after mixing for five minutes, and add one to two tablespoons of flour or water as needed.

Place the dough on a floured work space after the completion of its cycle and divide into halve.

Form the dough into a large ball and then flatten with the palm of your fingers.

When the dough is ready, place in two oiled nine-inch round pans. Cover the dough; let stand and increase its size for forty-five minutes.

Prepare the egg wash by beating the egg and water together and brush on top of dough. Sprinkle on top with optional Italian seasoning.

Bake for twenty to twenty-five minutes at 350 degrees Fahrenheit until golden brown.

Remove the bread from the pans and transfer to wire racks to completely cool.

Note: The time-delay feature of this machine is not recommended for this recipe.

Enjoy!

Nutritional Information: 87 calories; 2 g fat (1 g saturated fat); 22 mg cholesterol; 119 mg sodium; 15 g carbohydrate; 3 g total sugars; 0 g dietary fiber; 3 g protein.

Garlic Basil Bread

Each slice of this bread is composed of butter, sour cream, milk, Parmesan cheese, and flavored with basil and garlic. It is appealing to your taste buds, aside from its pleasing aroma and health benefits. You can have more slices because it is less sweet if you are on a diet.

Servings: 1 loaf (16 slices)

Ingredients

1/4 cup warm **(70° to 80°) sour cream**

2/3 cup warm **(70° to 80°) milk**

1 1/2 teaspoons **sugar**

1 tablespoon grated **Parmesan cheese**

1 tablespoon softened **butter**

1/2 teaspoon minced **garlic**

1 teaspoon **salt**

1/2 teaspoon **garlic powder**

1/2 teaspoon **dried basil**

3 cups **bread flour**

2 1/4 teaspoons **active dry yeast**

Directions

Put all ingredients in your bread machine according to its order.

Choose the basic bread setting, and then choose the crust color and then the size of loaf.

Bake the bread by carefully following the instructions of your machine, and inspect the dough after mixing for five minutes.

If possible add one to two tablespoons of flour or sugar if necessary.

Note: The time-delay feature of this machine is not recommended for this recipe.

Enjoy!

Nutritional Information: 100 calories; 2 g fat (1 g saturated fat); 6 mg cholesterol; 168 mg sodium; 18 g carbohydrate; 1 g total sugars; 1 g dietary fiber; 4 g protein.

GOLDEN WHEAT BREAD

The balance of sweetness and saltiness in this bread is just perfect for any type of jams, jelly, spreads, preserves or marmalade. It can go well with any type of drinks, such as fruit juice, milk or coffee. The crusty golden crust is a bonus to this awesome bread machine creation.

Servings: 1 loaf (1-1/2 pounds, 16 slices)

Ingredients

1 cup plus 2 tablespoons **(70° to 80°) water**

2 tablespoons **prepared mustard**

1/4 cup **canola oil**

1 teaspoon **salt**

2 tablespoons **honey**

1 cup **whole wheat flour**

2 1/2 cups **bread flour**

2 1/4 teaspoons **active dry yeast**

Directions

Put together all ingredients in a bread machine pan in the order instructed by the manufacturer.

Press basic bread setting and press the crust color and then press loaf size. Press start and bake based on the machine instructions.

Check the dough after mixing for five minutes.

Add in one to two tablespoons of flour or water if needed.

Serve!

Nutritional Information: 85 calorie; 3.7 g fat (0.3 g saturated fat); 0 mg cholesterol; 170 mg sodium; 11.7 g carbohydrate; 0.6 g dietary fiber; 2.4 g total sugars; 1.8 g protein.

HONEY OAT BREAD

Perk up your morning by having a mug of brewed coffee and two slices of this fantastic bread. It is flavored with oat and honey, which is good for your diabetic diet and it, can go along with pasta, soup or sandwiches.

Servings: 1 loaf (3/4 pound, 8 slices)

Ingredients

1/2 cup **(80° to 90°) water**

4 teaspoons **honey**

1 tablespoon **canola oil**

1/4 teaspoon **salt**

1/4 cup **quick-cooking oats**

2 1/4 teaspoons **bread machine** or **quick-rise yeast**

1 1/4 cups **bread flour**

Directions

Put all ingredients in a small bread machine pan in this order, water, canola oil, honey, salt, quick-cooking oats, bread flour, and yeast.

Choose the basic bread setting and start baking by following the machine instructions.

See to it that the dough is checked after mixing for five minutes, and then if needed, add at least one to two tablespoons of flour or dough.

Note: Never attempt to double the ingredients if you are using a bigger machine as this recipe can produce a ¾ pound loaf.

Serve!

Nutritional Information: 203 calorie; 4 g fat (0 g saturated fat); 0 mg cholesterol; 149 mg sodium; 37 g carbohydrate; 6 g total sugars; 2 g dietary fiber; 7 g protein.

TARRAGON CARROT BREAD

Healthy bread is not impossible with a bread machine pan. Try this bread flavored with carrot and tarragon. Honey is used to sweeten this tangy-moist and crunchy textured bread that is made with nonfat dry milk powder, All-Bran, whole wheat and bread flours.

Servings: 1 loaf, 16 slices (about 2 pounds)

Ingredients

1 cup plus 2 tablespoons **(70° to 80°) water**

2 tablespoons of **honey**

1 tablespoon **shortening**

3/4 cup **carrots**, grated

3 tablespoons of **instant nonfat dry milk powder**

2 tablespoons **dried tarragon**

1 1/2 teaspoons **orange zest**, grated

1 1/2 teaspoons **salt**

3/4 cup **All-Bran**

1 cup **whole wheat flour**

2 1/4 cups **bread flour**

1 1/4 teaspoons **active dry yeast**

Directions

Put together in a bread machine pan all ingredients beginning with water and ending up with yeast.

Choose the basic bread setting, and then choose the crust color and the loaf size.

Bake the bread based on the instructions of the bread machine.

After mixing the dough for 5 minutes, check it and then add in one to two tablespoons of flour or water.

Note: The time-delay feature of this machine is not recommended for this recipe.

Enjoy!

Nutritional Information: 128 calories; 1 g fat (0 g saturated fat); 1 mg cholesterol; 271 mg sodium; 26 g carbohydrate; 0 g total sugars; 0 g dietary fiber ; 5 g protein.

SUNFLOWER OATMEAL BREAD

If you want to add a nutty texture to your bread, try adding sunflower kernels in the bread mixture. For a moist and creamy taste, add butter, milk powder to your cooking oats and flour and sweeten the bread with honey. It is a perfect companion for your coffee. Toast the leftovers for your brunch.

Servings: 1 loaf (about 1-1/2 pounds)

Ingredients

1 cup plus 2 tablespoons **(70° to 80°) water**

1/4 cup **honey**

2 tablespoons softened **butter**

1 1/2 teaspoons **salt**

1/2 cup **quick-cooking oats**

3 cups **bread flour**

2 tablespoon of **nonfat dry milk powder**

2 1/4 teaspoons **active dry yeast**

1/2 cup **toasted salted sunflower kernels**

Directions

Place in a bread machine all ingredients beginning from water to sunflower kernels.

Press the basic bread setting. Press the crust color and then the loaf size. Begin baking by following the manufacturer's instructions.

Peek and see the dough after mixing for 5 minutes. If necessary, you may add 1 to 2 tablespoons of flour or water.

Serve!

Nutritional Information: 144 calories; 4 g fat (1 g saturated fat); 4 mg cholesterol; 267 mg sodium; 24 g carbohydrate; 5 g total sugars; 1 g dietary fiber; 5 g protein.

CORNMEAL MOLASSES BREAD

Turn your homemade bread into a family heirloom and to be passed on to the next generation. One of these recipes is Cornmeal Molasses Bread, made with the right combination of molasses as a sweetener and the cornmeal, flour and yeast for its nicely textured golden loaf.

Servings: 1 loaf (1-1/2 pounds)

Ingredients

1 cup **(70° to 80°) water**

1/4 cup **molasses**

1 tablespoon of **vegetable oil**

1/4 cup **cornmeal**

1/2 teaspoon **salt**

3 cups of **bread flour**

2 1/4 teaspoons **active dry yeast**

Directions

Put together all ingredients in the bread machine pan in a particular order and select the basic bread setting.

Press the button for crust color and the button for loaf size. Bake the bread as per machine instructions, making sure to inspect the dough after mixing for five minutes.

Pour one to two tablespoons of water or flour, if necessary.

Serve!

Nutritional Information: 106 calories; 1 g fat (0 g saturated fat); 0 mg cholesterol; 76 mg sodium; 22 g carbohydrate; 3 g total sugars; 1 g dietary fiber; 3 g protein.

Cappuccino Chip Bread

Coffee lovers should try making this coffee-flavored and vanilla flavored bread. All ingredients are baked together in a bread machine pan, and before the baking time lapse, add the miniature semisweet chocolate chips that make it a little bit sweet and gooey.

Servings: 1 loaf (1-1/2 pounds)

Ingredients

3/4 cup warm **(70° to 80°) milk**

1 **lightly beaten egg**

3 tablespoons of **instant coffee granules**

2 tablespoons **sugar**

2 tablespoons of **water**

1 tablespoon softened **butter**

3/4 teaspoon **salt**

1 teaspoon **vanilla extract**

3 cups **bread flour**

2 teaspoons **active dry yeast**

1/3 cup **miniature semisweet chocolate chips**

Directions

Place in order of appearance the ingredients excluding the miniature semisweet chocolate chips in the bread machine pan.

Press the basic bread setting. Press the crust color. Press the loaf size, in case your machine has.

Start baking as instructed in the bread machine manual, inspecting the dough after the ingredients are mixed for five minutes.

Add in one to two tablespoons of either water or flour.

When the machine signals the end of final kneading, add the semisweet chocolate chips to the machine.

Note: The time-delay feature of the bread machine is not advisable for this recipe.

Serve!

Nutritional Information: 120 calories; 3 g fat (1 g saturated fat); 17 mg cholesterol; 128 mg sodium; 21 g carbohydrate; 4 g total sugars; 1 g dietary fiber; 4 g protein.

SPICED RAISIN BREAD

This contest winning bread has captured the hearts of the judges because of its unique blend of ingredients to come up with a balanced sweetness and saltiness. It also boasts of its zesty flavor, crunchy texture and soft inside. It is loaded with spices and butter.

Servings: 1 loaf (1-1/2 pounds, 24 slices)

Ingredients

1 cup **(70° to 80°) water**

Additional 2 tablespoons **(70° to 80°) water**

3/4 cup **raisins**

2 tablespoons softened **butter**

2 tablespoons **brown sugar**

2 teaspoons **ground cinnamon**

1 teaspoon **salt**

1/4 teaspoon **ground nutmeg**

1/4 teaspoon **cloves ground**

1/4 teaspoon **orange zest grated**

3 cups **bread flour**

2 1/4 teaspoons **active dry yeast**

Directions

Prepare the bread machine pan by placing all ingredients in a particular order.

Press the basic bread setting. Press the crust color. Press the loaf size if it is available feature.

Start baking by following the instructions of the pan manual.

After the ingredients are all mixed for 5 minutes, try to check the dough and add 1 to 2 tablespoons of flour or water.

Note: The time-delay feature of the bread machine is not advisable for this recipe.

Serve!

Nutritional Information: 78 calories; 1 g fat (1 g saturated fat); 3 mg cholesterol; 106 mg sodium; 16 g carbohydrate; 4 g total sugars; 1 g dietary fiber; 2 g protein.

HONEY-WHEAT OATMEAL BREAD

Prepare this heavy oatmeal bread flavored with honey. The inside is a mixture of bread and wheat flours that gives it a dense, but soft texture. Its appearance looks so delicate, but its look could be deceiving. The bread is perfect for toast, sandwiches or spread with jam or jelly.

Servings: 1 loaf (2 pounds, 20 slices)

Ingredients

1 1/4 cups **(70° to 80°) water**

1/2 cup of **honey**

2 tablespoons **canola oil**

1 1/2 teaspoons **salt**

1 1/2 cups **bread flour**

1 1/2 cups **whole wheat flour**

1 cup **quick-cooking oats**

(1/4 ounces) 1 package **active dry yeast**

Directions

Place in a bread machine pan all ingredients by starting with water and ends with yeast.

Choose the basic bread setting. After this choose the crust color and then the loaf size.

Begin baking according to what is directed in the manual, checking the dough after the mixing is through.

Add in one to two tablespoons water or flour as needed.

Enjoy!

Nutritional Information: 115 calories; 2 g fat (0 g saturated fat); 0 mg cholesterol; 178 mg sodium; 23 g carbohydrate; 7 g total sugars; 2 g dietary fiber; 3 g protein.

DILL AND CHIVE BREAD

Give a boost to your plain bread by adding extra flavor from chive and onion cream cheese and dill weed. The taste would be more enhanced and the texture is unbelievably perfect; no need to spread the bread with marmalade or preserves.

Servings: 1 loaf (1-1/2 pounds, 16 slices)

Ingredients

3/4 cup (70° to 80°) **water**

1/2 cup of **spreadable chive and onion cream cheese**

2 tablespoons **sugar**

2 teaspoons **dill weed**

1 1/4 teaspoons **salt**

3 cups **all-purpose flour**

1 (1/4 ounce) package of **active dry yeast**

Directions

Put all ingredients in a bread machine pan according to its particular order from water to yeast.

Choose the setting for basic bread, and crust color and lastly the loaf size.

Begin baking according to the manual instructions.

Inspect the dough after mixing is finished for five minutes.

Add a tablespoon or more of water or flour if you think it is needed.

Enjoy!

Nutritional Information: 121 calories; 3 g fat (2 g saturated fat); 8 mg cholesterol; 219 mg sodium; 20 g carbohydrate; 2 g total sugars; 1 g dietary fiber; 3 g protein.

THREE-SEED BREAD

This bread derived its name from the three seeds added to the ingredients for a nutty and crunchy texture. They include sesame seeds, poppy seeds and sesame seeds. The bread is sweetened with honey and its creaminess is courtesy of butter and nonfat dry milk powder.

Servings: 1 loaf (1 pound)

Ingredients

2/3 cup plus 2 teaspoons (**70° to 80°**) **water**

1 tablespoon softened **butter**

1 tablespoon of **honey**

2 tablespoons **sunflower kernels**

2 tablespoons **sesame seeds**

2 tablespoons **poppy seeds**

3/4 teaspoon **salt**

1 cup **whole wheat flour**

1 cup **bread flour**

3 tablespoons of **nonfat dry milk powder**

2 teaspoons **active dry yeast**

Directions

Put all ingredients in a bread machine pan according to its order, beginning with water and ends with dry yeast.

Choose the basic bread setting and then choose the crust color and then the loaf size, if this feature is available.

Read carefully the instruction manual and start baking.

Check the dough right away when mixing is finished and then, if it is too thick, add water or if it is too thin, add flour.

Baking time is between 3 to four hours.

Serve!

Nutritional Information: 84 calories; 2 g fat (1 g saturated fat); 2 mg cholesterol; 133 mg sodium; 14 g carbohydrate; 2 g total sugars; 1 g dietary fiber; 3 g protein.

SOUR CREAM LEMON BREAD

Treat yourself with this contest winning bread that has an extra creaminess and zesty hint. This lip-smacking bread is ideal for any meal from breakfast to midnight snack, which everyone will surely love due to its soft-light texture that can feed a throng of people.

Servings: 1 loaf (1 pound) and about 1/2 cup spread3

Ingredients

2 tablespoons **lemon juice**

1/4 cup **sour cream**

2 to 3 tablespoons **warm (70° to 80°) whole milk**

2 tablespoons softened **butter**

1 large **egg**

2 teaspoons **lemon zest**, grated

2 tablespoons **sugar**

1 teaspoon **salt**

1/4 teaspoon **baking soda**

2 cups **bread flour**

1 1/2 teaspoons **active dry yeast**

For the lemon spread:

3 ounces softened **cream cheese**

1/4 cup **confectioners' sugar**

1 tablespoon of **lemon juice**

1 teaspoon **lemon zest**, grated

Directions

Combine the lemon juice and sour cream in a measuring cup, adding enough milk to come up with ½ cup.

Place in a bread machine pan the sour cream mixture, followed by the butter, egg, lemon zest, 2 tablespoons sugar, 1 teaspoon salt, ¼ teaspoon baking soda, bread flour and active dry yeast.

Choose the sweet bread setting. Choose the crust color and the loaf size, and then start baking as directed by the manual.

Check the dough when everything is mixed for five minutes. If it is necessary to add flour or water, add a tablespoon or more.

Combine in a small bowl the ingredients for the spread, whisking until it becomes smooth. Serve the bread with spread.

Note: Using the time-delay feature of the bread machine is not recommended for this recipe.

In case, your machine does not have a setting for sweet bread, use the basic setting instead as per directed in the manual.

Enjoy!

Nutritional Information: 110 calories; 4 g fat (3 g saturated fat); 26 mg cholesterol; 204 mg sodium; 15 g carbohydrate; 4 g total sugars; 1 g dietary fiber; 3 g protein.

HARVEST FRUIT BREAD

This fruit and nut studded bread is probably the best when it comes to its nutty texture. This is because the bread is packed with ground nutmeg, chopped pecans and dried mixed fruit with the infusion of allspice and moistened by egg and butter.

Servings: 1 loaf (12 slices)

Ingredients

1 cup plus 2 tablespoons **(70° to 80°) water**

1 **egg**

3 tablespoons softened **butter**

1/4 cup **packed brown sugar**

1 1/2 teaspoons **salt**

1/4 teaspoon **ground nutmeg**

Dash **allspice**

3 3/4 cups **bread flour**

Additional 1 tablespoon **bread flour**

2 teaspoons **active dry yeast**

1 cup dried **mixed fruit (dried cherries, dried cranberries or raisins)**

1/3 cup chopped **pecans**

Directions

Put together in the bread machine pan the first 9 ingredients beginning with water and ending with the yeast.

Press basic bread setting. Press crust color and then loaf size.

Bake the bread according to the manual's directions, checking the dough when mixing is finished after five minutes.

Look carefully at the dough and see if it needs additional tablespoon of flour or water.

When the machine signals that it's almost done with final kneading, add the mixed dried fruits and pecans.

Note: The time-delay feature of the bread machine is not recommended for this recipe.

Serve!

Nutritional Information: 214 calories; 6 g fat (2 g saturated fat); 25 mg cholesterol; 330 mg sodium; 36 g carbohydrate; 0 total sugars; 2 g dietary fiber); 6 g protein.

MOIST WILD RICE BREAD

Give life to your sandwiches by preparing this old-fashioned styled-bread. It is given a twist by adding rice to the dough before the final kneading ends. The bread is sweetened with molasses and its fragrant aroma comes from the dried rosemary.

Servings: 1 loaf (1-1/2 pounds)

Ingredients

1 cup **warm (70° to 80°) water**

4 1/2 teaspoons **canola oil**

4 1/2 teaspoons **molasses**

1 1/2 teaspoons **salt**

2 3/4 cups **bread flour**

1 teaspoon crushed **dried rosemary**

1 3/4 teaspoons **active dry yeast**

3/4 cup **cooked wild rice** or **Vegetable Wild Rice**

Directions

Place altogether in a bread machine pan the first 7 ingredients in their particular order.

Choose the basic bread setting, choose crust color, and choose loaf size.

Bake the dough according to the manual instructions and don't forget to check on the dough after mixing for five minutes.

Add in one to two tablespoons of either flour or water, if needed.

Add the rice to the mixture a few minutes before its final kneading. Be sensitive to the signal given by the machine.

Nutritional Information: 94 calories; 1 g fat (0 g saturated fat); 0 mg cholesterol; 222 mg sodium; 18 g carbohydrate; 1 g total sugars; 1 g dietary fiber; 3 g protein.

Rolls

Frosted Cinnamon Rolls

These contest winning rolls are absolutely the best when it comes to its taste and texture. The dough is sprinkled with butter; brown sugar and cinnamon and then rolled before baking. The baked rolls are topped with vanilla-flavored cream cheese frosting.

Servings: 21 rolls

Ingredients

1 cup **warm (70° to 80°) milk**

1/4 cup **(70° to 80°) water**

1/4 cup softened **butter**

1 large **egg**

1 teaspoon **salt**

4 cups **bread flour**

1/4 cup of **instant vanilla pudding mix**

1 tablespoon **sugar**

1 tablespoon **active dry yeast**

For the filling:

1/4 cup softened **butter**

2 teaspoons **ground cinnamon**

1 cup **brown sugar, packed**

For the frosting:

1/4 cup softened **butter**

1 1/2 cups **confectioners' sugar**

1 1/2 teaspoons **milk**

1/2 teaspoon of **vanilla extract**

4 ounces softened **cream cheese**

Directions

Place in a bread machine pan the first 9 ingredients in this order: milk, water, butter, egg, salt, flour, vanilla pudding mix, sugar and active dry yeast.

Choose the dough setting and check right away after the dough are mixed for five minutes, adding at least one to two tablespoons of flour or water if really needed.

Place the dough on a floured work surface when the cycle is over.

Roll the dough into a 17"by10" rectangle and spread on top with butter, and sprinkle with brown sugar and ground cinnamon.

Roll up the dough to resemble a jelly roll beginning from its long side and then pinch the seam to lightly seal.

Cut the rolls into 21 equal sizes and place in a greased 13by9-inch baking pan, cut side down and place nine rolls in a 9-inch square baking pan; cover and let rise for forty-five minutes in a warm place.

Place both pans in the oven and bake for 20 to 25 minutes at 350 degrees F. Let cool for ten minutes on wire racks.

Prepare the frosting by beating all ingredients until smooth and frost the warm rolls. Keep refrigerated.

The time-delay feature of the bread machine is not recommended for this recipe.

Enjoy!

Nutritional Information: 266 calories; 10 g fat (6 g saturated fat); 33 mg cholesterol; 208 mg sodium; 41 g carbohydrate; 21 g total sugars; 1 g dietary fiber; 4 g protein.

CHERRY-PECAN STREUSEL ROLLS

These baking contest winning sweet streusel rolls can be done in twenty minutes in a bread machine pan. The filling is given extra sweetness by the addition of dried tart cherries aside from its nutty texture from pecans and flavored with cinnamon. The baked rolls are drizzled with almond-milk extract.

Servings: 12 rolls

Ingredients

1/2 cup **warm (70° to 80°) 2% milk**

1/4 cup melted **butter**

1/4 cup **sugar**

1 large **egg**

1/2 teaspoon **salt**

1 3/4 cups **all-purpose flour**

2/3 cup **quick-cooking oats**

2 1/4 teaspoons **bread machine yeast**

For the filling:

1/2 cup **sugar**

2/3 cup chopped **pecans**

1/3 cup melted **butter**

1/3 cup **quick-cooking oats**

1 1/2 teaspoons **ground cinnamon**

1/3 cup finely chopped **almond paste**

1/2 cup chopped **dried tart cherries**

2 tablespoons **all-purpose flour**

For the glaze:

1 cup **confectioners' sugar**

4 teaspoons **2% milk**

1/4 teaspoon **almond extract**

Directions

Place in a bread machine pan the first 8 ingredients in this order: milk, butter, sugar, egg, salt, flour, oats and yeasts.

Press dough setting and check the dough after it was mixed for five minutes.

Add one to two tablespoons of flour or water to the machine pan if needed.

Transfer the dough onto a slightly floured surface when the cycle has completed.

Roll the dough to form into a 16inchby8 inch-rectangle.

Combine in a small bowl the sugar, pecans, butter, oats and cinnamon, setting aside 1/3 cup for the topping.

Stir the remaining filling in almond paste and cherries: sprinkle on top of dough at least one-fourth" of its edges.

Start rolling up the dough to resemble a jelly roll. Start with the long side and pinch the seam to seal.

Cut the rolls into twelve slices and neatly arrange in your greased 13"by9" baking pan with cut side down. Cover the pan and let stand for 1 hour until the size has doubled.

Preheat the oven at 340 degrees Fahrenheit.

Add flour to the reserved topping and stir to combine; pour over the rolls. Bake for twenty to twenty-five minutes until golden brown.

Beat in a small bowl the confectioner's sugar, extract and milk until smooth and drizzle over the baked rolls.

Serve!

Nutritional Information: 370 calories; 17 g fat (7 g saturated fat); 42 mg cholesterol; 174 mg sodium; 51 g carbohydrate; 28 g total sugars; 3 g dietary fiber; 6 g protein.

Golden Honey Pan Rolls

These highly enjoyable honey-glazed rolls are time savers. Instead of baking for several hours, you can do it for two hours in a bread machine. These rolls received a prize for winning in the rolls category and the secret lies on its devilishly delicious and buttery taste.

Servings: 2 dozens

Ingredients

1 cup **warm (70° to 80°) 2% milk**

1 large **egg**

1 large **egg yolk**

1/2 cup **canola oil**

2 tablespoons **honey**

1 1/2 teaspoons **salt**

3 1/2 cups **bread flour**

2 1/4 teaspoons **active dry yeast**

For the glaze:

1/3 cup **sugar**

2 tablespoons melted **butter**

1 tablespoon **honey plus extra honey**

1 large **egg white**

Directions

Place the first 8 ingredients in its particular order and select the dough setting, checking the dough after five minutes of mixing.

Add one to two tablespoons of flour or water to the mixture if necessary.

Once the cycle has completed, divide the dough into twenty-four pieces and form into individual balls.

Grease two 8" square baking pans and arrange the twelve balls on each pan; cover and let stand in a warm place for thirty minutes until the size has doubled.

Prepare the glaze by combining the butter, sugar, egg white, and honey.

Drizzle the glaze over the dough and bake for 20 to 25 minutes at 350 degrees F.

Brush the rolls with extra honey for extra sweetness.

Note: The time-delay feature of the bread machine is not recommended for this recipe.

Serve!

Nutritional Information: 139 calories; 6 g fat (2 g saturated fat); 22 mg cholesterol; 168 mg sodium; 18 g carbohydrate; 5 g total sugars;, 1 g dietary fiber; 3 g protein.

GARLIC-HERB PARMESAN ROLLS

These tree-shaped rolls could feed more than a dozen people. It will surely capture everyone's heart with its array of seasonings and brushed with butter and then sprinkled with a blend of Italian seasoning and Parmesan cheese. It will be ready in a total of 40 minutes.

Servings: 16 servings

Ingredients

1 cup **warm (70° to 80°) water**

2 tablespoons softened **butter**

1 large lightly **beaten egg**

3 tablespoons **sugar**

2 teaspoons dried minced **garlic**

1 teaspoon **Italian seasoning**

1 teaspoon **salt**

2 1/4 cups **bread flour**

1 cup **whole wheat flour**

1 package (1/4 ounce) **active dry yeast**

For the topping:

1 tablespoon melted **butter**

1 teaspoon **Italian seasoning**

1 tablespoon **Parmesan cheese**, grated

1/2 teaspoon **coarse salt**

Directions

Put together in a bread machine pan the first ten ingredients beginning with water and ends with yeast.

Select the dough setting, check the dough when everything is mixed after five minutes and it is up to you to add one to two tablespoons of flour or water if needed.

Once the cycle is already complete, transfer the dough onto a floured surface and divide into sixteen balls.

Cover the bottom of a large baking sheet with foil and coat the foil with oil.

Place one roll in the center near the topmost part of the sheet. Arrange the rolls side by side to form into 4 additional rows and add another roll per row to resemble a tree. Just imagine that you are building a tree using the rolls. Put one ball in the center, just below the triangle to form the trunk of the tree. Cover the rolls and let rise for 1 hour.

Lightly brush the rolls with butter.

Mix together the Italian seasoning and Parmesan cheese; sprinkle on top of rolls, and then sprinkle with a little amount of salt.

Bake for twenty to twenty-five minutes at 350 degrees F until the rolls are golden brown. Serve immediately.

Enjoy!

Nutritional Information: 78 calorie; 2.5 g fat (1.3 g saturated fat); 16 mg cholesterol; 229 mg sodium; 11.6 g carbohydrate; 0.3 g dietary fiber; 2.5 g total sugars; 2 g protein.

SEASONED PARMESAN ROLLS

Prepare these delicious bread rolls that can be baked in 20 minutes in a bread machine pan. The cheesy soft rolls are flavored with seafood seasoning. The rolls are cheesy, flavorful and buttery due to the perfect blend of milk, butter, Parmesan cheese and dried onion.

Servings: 2 dozens

Ingredients

1 1/2 cups **warm (70° to 80°) milk**

2 tablespoons softened **butter**

1 tablespoon **sugar**

1/2 cup **Parmesan cheese grated**

1 tablespoon **dried onion**, minced

2 teaspoons **seafood seasoning**

4 cups **bread flour**

4 teaspoons **active dry yeast**

Directions

Place in a bread machine pan all ingredients in a particular order.

Choose the dough setting and never forget to check the dough after mixing for five minutes and check if it needs an addition of 1 to 2 tablespoons of flour or water.

Turn the dough on a floured surface when the cycle has completed.

Divide the dough into 24 equal sizes and form into a ball.

Arrange the balls on buttered baking sheets, at least three inches apart. Cover the sheets for thirty minutes until the size of balls has doubled.

Bake the balls for fifteen to twenty minutes at 350 degrees F. Let cool on wire racks.

Note: The time-delay feature of the bread machine is not recommended for this recipe.

Serve!

Nutritional Information: 105 calories; 2 g fat (1 g saturated fat); 4 mg cholesterol; 33 mg sodium; 18 g carbohydrate; 0 g total sugars; 1 g dietary fiber; 4 g protein.

GARLIC HOAGIE ROLLS

The golden crunchy crust of these rolls and its soft, creamy texture are remarkably the best. These submarine rolls can be finished in thirty-minute including the preparation, baking and cooling. The rolls are great for toasts, sandwiches and can be paired with chocolate drinks, milk or coffee.

Servings: 9 rolls

Ingredients

1/2 cup of **warm (70° to 80°) water**

1/2 cup **warm (70° to 80°) 2% milk**

1 lightly beaten **egg**

2 tablespoons **sugar**

1 tablespoon softened **butter**

1 tablespoon **chives**, minced

1/2 teaspoon **salt**

1/2 teaspoon **garlic salt**

3 1/4 cups **bread flour**

3 teaspoons **active dry yeast**

Directions

Put together all ingredients in a bread machine pan in its order of appearance as suggested by the manufacturer.

Choose the dough setting, checking the dough when mixing is completed after five minutes and adding 1 to 2 tablespoons flour or water if necessary.

Turn the dough on a slightly floured work surface once the cycle is completed.

Divide the dough into nine equal portions and form into a 4 ½" by 1 ½" rolls.

Neatly arrange the rolls on oiled baking sheets, about four inches apart. Cover the baking sheets and let the dough increase its size for 20 to 30 minutes.

Bake for 12 to 15 minutes at 375 degrees F until nicely golden brown.

Remove the rolls from the baking sheets and let cool on wire racks.

Note: It is not recommended for this recipe to use the time-delay feature of the bread machine.

Enjoy!

Nutritional Information: 187 calories; 2 g fat (1 g saturated fat); 28 mg cholesterol; 255 mg sodium; 36 g carbohydrate; 3 g total sugars; 1 g dietary fiber; 7 g protein.

Focaccia
Sun-Dried Tomato Focaccia

After getting tired of the same bread recipes, it is about time to shift to focaccia. This recipe offers the best of your focaccia; it is crunchy outside but soft inside. The slivered sun-dried tomatoes and onion slices, add appeal to the focaccia loaves, which makes it a perfect treat for celebrations.

Servings: 2 loaves (8 servings each)

Ingredients

1/2 cup **boiling water**

1/4 cup chopped (not packed in oil) **sun-dried tomatoes**

1 1/4 cups **warm (70° to 80°) V8 juice**

2 tablespoons of **olive oil**

1/4 cup **Parmesan cheese**, grated

1 tablespoon **dried parsley flakes**

2 teaspoons **sugar**

1 teaspoon **salt**

1 teaspoon **dried basil**

1/2 teaspoon **garlic powder**

2 cups **whole wheat flour**

1 1/2 cups **all-purpose flour**

2 teaspoons **active dry yeast**

For the topping:

1/4 cup **boiling water**

2 tablespoons (not packed in oil) **slivered sun-dried tomatoes**

12 thin slices **red onion**, halved

1 tablespoon **olive oil**

Directions

Stir in a small bowl the chopped sun-dried tomatoes in boiling water, let stand for five minutes and drain.

Meanwhile, place in your bread machine pan the V8 juice, olive oil, Parmesan cheese, parsley flakes, sugar, salt, dried basil, garlic powder, wheat flour, all-purpose flour and yeast.

Choose the dough setting and inspect the dough right after mixing for five minutes and then add water or flour about 1 to 2 tablespoons if needed.

Stir in a small bowl the slivered tomatoes in boiling water; let stand for five minutes, drain and pat dry using a clean dishcloth or paper towels.

Transfer the dough when it has completed the cycle onto a lightly floured work surface. Slightly punch down and divide into halve. Roll into a nine-inch circle.

Coat two 9-inches round baking pans with oil and place the dough. Make a 1/4-inch hollow in the dough by using the end of the wooden spoon handle.

Place the onion slices and tomato slivers on top of the dough, pressing down lightly. Cover the pans and let the dough double its size for thirty minutes in a warm place.

Brush the dough with oil and bake for 20 to 25 minutes at 375 degrees F until nicely golden brown.

Remove the Focaccia from pan and let cool on wire racks.

Serve!

Nutritional Information: 135 calories; 3 g fat (1 g saturated fat); 1 mg cholesterol; 247 mg sodium; 23 g carbohydrate; 2 g total sugars; 3 g dietary fiber; 4 g protein.

CHEESY ONION FOCACCIA

Treat your family with this aromatic focaccia flavored with onion, Parmesan and cheddar. Their top golden brown crusts are enjoyable to munch over a cup of your favorite coffee flavor. You need 1 hour to prepare the focaccia and 15 minutes of baking time.

Servings: 12

Ingredients

3/4 cup **warm (70° to 80°) water**

2 tablespoons **olive oil**

1 teaspoon **salt**

2 cups **bread flour**

1 tablespoon **sugar**

1 1/2 teaspoons **active dry yeast**

2 medium quartered and sliced **onions**

1/4 cup **butter**

3 minced **garlic cloves**

2 teaspoons **Italian seasoning**

1 cup **cheddar cheese**, shredded

2 tablespoons **Parmesan cheese**, grated

Directions

Place in a bread machine the warm water, olive oil, salt, bread flour, sugar and active dry yeast.

Choose the dough setting and check the dough after mixing for five minutes. Add in one to two tablespoons of flour or water if necessary.

Grease a twelve-inch pizza pan and place the dough when the cycle is completed. Pat the dough into a ten-inch circle; cover and let rise for half an hour in a warm place, until the size has doubled.

Melt the butter in a large pan and sauté the onions until fragrant and soft. Cook on medium low heat, stirring often, for thirty minutes until dark golden brown.

Pour the Italian seasoning and stir together with the garlic; cook for one minute more.

Create a deep depression about 1-inch apart in the dough by using the end of your wooden spoon handle.

Arrange the cheeses and onions on top of the dough. Bake for fifteen to eighteen at 400 degree Fahrenheit until golden brown. Serve hot.

Enjoy!

Nutritional Information: 174 calories; 9 g fat (5 g saturated fat); 21 mg cholesterol; 309 mg sodium; 19 g carbohydrate; 3 g total sugars; 1 g dietary fiber; 6 g protein.

Rosemary Garlic Focaccia

Make your dinner extra special by having this savory focaccia along with your pasta dish. It is perfect for someone who loves garlic and rosemary. Each bite is creamylicious with the goodness of 2% milk and butter. It requires 45 minutes of preparation plus rising and 15 minutes baking time.

Servings: 2 loaves (10 wedges each)

Ingredients

1 cup **warm (70° to 80°) 2% milk**

1 **egg**

1/4 cup of **warm (70° to 80°) water**

1/4 cup softened **butter**

2 3/4 cups **bread flour**

2 tablespoons **sugar**

1 teaspoon **salt**

2 tsp. **active dry yeast**

4 teaspoons **olive oil**

4 teaspoons **fresh rosemary**, minced

3 **garlic cloves**, minced

1 teaspoon **kosher salt**

Directions

Place in a bread machine pan the milk, egg, warm water, butter, bread flour, sugar, salt and active dry yeast.

Choose the dough setting, check the dough when mixing is finished for five minutes, and add one to two tablespoons water or flour if necessary.

Place the dough on top of a lightly floured work surface when the cycle reaches its completion.

Divide the dough into two parts and place them on greased baking sheets. Cover the sheets for ten minutes to let the dough rest, and then form into an eight-inch circle.

Cover the dough and let stand to double its size for thirty minutes.

Create a one-fourth-inch depression in the dough with the help of a wooden spoon handle.

Brush the dough with oil. Sprinkle on top with minced rosemary, minced garlic and salt.

Bake for twelve to fifteen minutes at 400 degrees F until golden brown. Let cool on wire racks.

Serve!

Nutritional Information: 101 calories; 4 g fat (2 g saturated fat); 18 mg cholesterol; 237 mg sodium; 14 g carbohydrate; 2 g total sugars; 1 g dietary fiber; 3 g protein.

Vegetable & Cheese Focaccia

This focaccia does not only look attractive, but it is packed with nutrients from its toppings consisting of basil, tomatoes, onion, and broccoli. The cheesy golden crust complements with its soft inside flavored with dried oregano. You will only need 20 minutes of preparing plus rising and 30 minutes of baking time.

Servings: 15 slices

Ingredients

1 cup **warm (70° to 80°) water**

4 1/2 teaspoons **olive oil**

4 1/2 teaspoons **sugar**

2 teaspoons **dried oregano**

1 1/4 teaspoons **salt**

3 1/4 cups **bread flour**

1 1/2 teaspoons **active dry yeast**

Topping:

1 tablespoon **olive oil**

1 tablespoon **dried basil**

2 medium thinly sliced **tomatoes**

1 medium thinly sliced **onion**

1 cup frozen thawed chopped **broccoli**

1/4 teaspoon **salt**

1/4 teaspoon **pepper**

3/4 cup **Parmesan cheese**, grated

1 cup **part-skim mozzarella cheese**, shredded

Directions

Place in a bread machine pan the first 7 ingredients in a particular order, beginning with water and ending up in active dry yeast.

Opt for the dough setting and check the dough after mixing for 5 minutes. Try to peek if it needs additional flour or water at least 1 to 2 tablespoons.

Transfer the dough on a flour-dusted work surface when the cycle is completed.

Punch the dough down and roll into a 13by9-inch rectangle and then transfer to a greased baking dish with the same size of the dough.

Brush the dough with olive oil and sprinkle with fresh basil.

Place on top of the basil the sliced tomatoes, sliced onion, chopped broccoli, and sprinkle with salt, pepper and then the Parmesan cheese. Cover the dough for thirty minutes until the size has doubled.

Bake for twenty minutes at 350 degrees F. Sprinkle on top with mozzarella cheese and bake for ten to fifteen minutes until the cheese has melted and the focaccia is golden brown.

Enjoy!

Nutritional Information: 151 calories; 4 g fat (2 g saturated fat); 7 mg cholesterol; 315 mg sodium; 22 g carbohydrate; 3 g total sugars; 2 g dietary fiber; 7 g protein.

HERBED PARMESAN ONION FOCACCIA

You don't need to spread this focaccia with marmalade or butter as it is loaded with seasonings, sugar, salt, cheese and herbs. The cheesy and flaky topping will impress your guests and you'll be congratulated for a job well done.

Servings: 1 loaf (1-1/2 pounds, 16 slices)

Ingredients

1 cup **(70° to 80°) water**

1/3 cup **onion**, finely chopped

1 tablespoon **sugar**

1 1/2 teaspoons **salt**

1 teaspoon **Parmesan cheese**, grated

1/2 teaspoon **garlic powder**

1/2 teaspoon **dried basil**

1/2 teaspoon **dill weeds**

1/2 teaspoon **pepper**

3 cups **all-purpose flour**

2 teaspoons **active dry yeast**

Topping:

1 tablespoon **olive oil**

1/2 teaspoon **Parmesan cheese**, grated

1/2 teaspoon **dried parsley flakes**

1/4 teaspoon **salt**

1/8 teaspoon **pepper**

Directions

Place in a bread machine pan the first eleven ingredients starting with 1 cup of water and ending up with 2 teaspoons of active dry yeast.

Select the dough setting, check the dough when the mixing is completed after five minutes. Pour 1 to 2 tablespoons water or flour to the mixture if needed.

Take note when the cycle has reached its completion and transfer the dough on a lightly greased baking sheet.

Punch down and pat the dough using your oiled hands into a nine-inch circle; brush the dough with oil.

Sprinkle on top with grated Parmesan cheese, dried parsley flakes, salt and pepper; cover for 45 minutes until the dough has doubled its size in a warm place.

Bake for eighteen to twenty minutes at 400 degrees F until golden brown. Cut the focaccia into wedges.

Enjoy!

Nutritional Information: 100 calories; 1 g fat (0 g fat); 0 mg cholesterol; 262 mg sodium; 19 g carbohydrate; 1 g total sugars, 1 g dietary fiber; 3 g protein.

BAGELS
CRANBERRY ORANGE BAGELS

Delight your picky eater kids with sweet, tangy bagels flavored with dried cranberries and with a hint of orange. The bagels are brushed with egg washed before baking. Your kids will love to bring these tasty bagels to school too.

Servings: 9 bagels

Ingredients

1 cup plus 4 tablespoons **(70° to 80°) water**, divided

1/2 cup **dried cranberries**

1/3 cup **packed brown sugar**

4 1/2 teaspoons of **orange zest**, grated

1 teaspoon **salt**

1/4 teaspoon **ground cloves**

3 cups **bread flour**

1 package **active dry yeast** (1/4 ounce)

1 tablespoon **sugar**

1 large **egg white**

1 tablespoon **cornmeal**

Directions

Put in a bread machine pan the water, dried cranberries, packed brown sugar; grated orange zest, salt, ground cloves, bread flour and active dry yeast.

Choose the dough setting (checking the dough when mixing is completed after five minutes); and then add water or flour at least 1 to 2 tablespoons if necessary.

When the cycle is finished, place the dough on a flour-dusted surface and form into nine balls, pushing your thumb through the centers to create a one-inch hole.

Stretch the dough and form into an even ring; cover for ten minutes to rest and then slightly flatten out the rings.

Prepare a Dutch oven by filling with 2/3 full water. Add in the sugar and let boil.

Drop two bagels at a time into the boiling water and cook for forty-five seconds. Flip and cook for another 45 seconds; remove using a slotted spoon and drain to remove excess liquid.

Meanwhile, whisk the egg white in remaining water and brush the bagels.

Spray a baking sheet with cooking spray, and dust with cornmeal. Arrange the bagels on the pan about two inches apart.

Bake for eighteen to twenty-two minutes at 400 degrees F until golden brown. Let cool on wire racks.

Note: It is not recommended to use the time-delay feature of the bread machine for this recipe.

Enjoy!

Nutritional Information: 197 calories; 0 fat (0 g saturated fat); 0 mg cholesterol; 272 mg sodium; 45 g carbohydrate; 13 g total sugars; 2 g dietary fiber; 6 g protein.

Pumpkin Spice Bagels

These tantalizing bagels are great for breakfast, brunch or dinner. Each bagel is packed with four spices and flavored with pumpkin. The egg wash adds luster to the sweet golden crust of these bagels that can be finished in 45 minutes.

Servings: 9

Ingredients

2/3 cup plus 2 tablespoons **(70° to 80°) water**, divided

1/2 cup **pumpkin**, canned

1/3 cup **brown sugar packed**

1 teaspoon **salt**

3/4 teaspoon **ground nutmeg**

1/2 teaspoon **ground allspice**

1 1/2 teaspoons **ground cinnamon**

1/2 teaspoon **ground cloves**

3 cups **bread flour**

1 package **active dry yeast** (1/4 ounce)

1 **egg white**

1 tablespoon **cornmeal**

Directions

Place in a bread machine pan the 2/3 cups of water, ½ cup pumpkin, 1/3 cup brown sugar, 1 teaspoon salt, ground nutmeg, ground allspice, ground cinnamon, ground cloves, bread flour and yeast.

Select the dough setting. Check the dough after mixing for five minutes, and if there is a need for additional flour or water, add 1 to 2 tablespoons.

Place the dough on a lightly flour dusted surface when the cycle is completed.

Shape the dough into nine ball pieces, pushing your thumb through the center to create a one-inch hole. Stretch the dough and form into a ring. Cover the dough and let it rest for ten minutes and slightly flatten.

Fill your Dutch oven with 2/3 full of water, let boil and drop two bagels at a time. Cook the bagels for 45 seconds per side, flipping once to cook the other side.

Using a slotted spoon, remove the bagels and drain on a clean dishcloth or paper towels.

Whisk in a small bowl the egg white with the remaining 2 tablespoons of water and brush the egg wash on bagels.

Grease a baking sheet and dust with cornmeal. Arrange the bagels on the pan, two inches apart.

Bake for 15 to 20 minutes at 400 degrees F. Remove from oven when it becomes golden brown and let cool on wire racks.

Note: It is not advisable to use the time-delay feature of the bread machine for this recipe.

Serve!

Nutritional Information: 180 calories; 0 g fat (0 g saturated fat); 0 mg cholesterol; 273 mg sodium; 40 g carbohydrate; 8 g total sugars; 2 g dietary fiber; 6 g protein.

NAAN

BREAD MACHINE NAAN

This Asian flatbread is what you need if you are watching your diet. It uses 2% milk, plain yogurt and milk in addition to the flour, yeast and baking powder. Although it is sweetened with sugar, it is less sweet due to the presence of salt, as a neutralizer. It is best served with your favorite Indian dish.

Servings: 6

Ingredients

3/4 cup **warm (70° to 80°) 2% milk**

3/4 cup **plain yogurt** (about 6 ounces)

1 large beaten **egg**

2 tablespoons **canola oil**

1 teaspoon **salt**

2 teaspoons **sugar**

1 teaspoon **baking powder**

4 cups **bread flour**

2 teaspoons **active dry yeast**

Directions

Place all ingredients in a bread machine pan starting with 2% milk and ends with active dry yeast.

Opt for the dough setting. Make sure to check the dough after the ingredients are mixed together for five minutes. Try to see if it needs an addition of water or flour at least 1 to 2 tablespoons.

Wait for the cycle to complete and remove the dough onto a floured surface.

Divide the dough into six parts and shape them into balls.

Roll the balls into one-fourth-inch thick oval, let stand for five minutes, and brush the tops with water.

Cover and cook the dough in a large oiled skillet with the wet side facing down for one minute on medium high heat. Flip, cover and cook for thirty seconds until it turns golden brown.

Repeat with the same procedure for the remaining dough.

Serve!

Nutritional Information: 363 calories; 7 g fat (2 g saturated fat), 42 mg cholesterol; 502 mg sodium; 64 g carbohydrate; 4 g total sugars; 2 g dietary fiber; 14 g protein.

FLATBREAD

CINNAMON FLATBREAD

This molasses sweetened flatbread is so easy to prepare, and ideal for busy people like you. The bread is a perfect blend of milk, butter, wheat germ, yeast and flour. You find yourself licking the buttery, crunchy top part, which is sprinkled with sugar and cinnamon. Baking time takes half an hour only.

Servings: 16 wedges*Ingredients*

1 cup **warm (70° to 80°) water**

2 tablespoons **butter**

2 tablespoons of **nonfat dry milk powder**

1 tablespoon **sugar**

1 1/2 teaspoons **salt**

1 tablespoon **wheat germ**, toasted

2 teaspoons **molasses**

3 cups **all-purpose flour**

2 1/4 teaspoons of **active dry yeast**

Topping:

3 tablespoons softened **butter**

1 teaspoon **ground cinnamon**

1/2 cup **packed brown sugar**

Directions

Place all ingredients in a bread machine pan, excluding the topping ingredients. Start it with water up to the dry active yeast.

Select the bread dough setting. Check also the dough when mixing is finished after five minutes. Decide whether to add 1 to 2 tablespoons of flour or water based on the consistency of the dough.

It is time to transfer the dough when the cycle is completed, to a lightly floured work surface.

Now roll the dough into 14-inch circle and place in a 14-inch pizza pan coated with oil.

Create a dent over the dough using your fingers. Spread on top of dent the butter, and sprinkle with packed brown sugar and ground cinnamon.

Cover the dough with plastic for twenty-five minutes to let it rise until the size has doubled. Bake for half an hour at 375 degrees F until golden brown. Let cool for five minutes.

Cut the flatbread into wedges. Serve immediately.

Enjoy!

Nutritional Information: 155 calories; 4 g fat (2 g saturated fat); 10 mg cholesterol; 266 mg sodium; 27 g carbohydrate; 9 g total sugars; 1 g dietary fiber; 3 g protein.

Loaf
Cheddar Olive Loaf

Enjoy unlimited slices of this loaf bread flavored with pimiento-stuffed olives. It's moist inside and crusty outside that is a perfect breakfast buddy to perk up your day. It is not so sweet and its cheesy taste makes it a big hit at your dinner table.

Servings: 1 loaf (1-1/2 pounds, 16 slices)

Ingredients

1 cup **warm (70° to 80°) water**

4 teaspoons **sugar**

3/4 teaspoon **salt**

1 1/4 cups **shredded sharp cheddar cheese**

3 cups **bread flour**

2 teaspoons **active dry yeast**

3/4 cup well drained and sliced **pimiento-stuffed olives**

Directions

Place in a bread machine pan the first 6 ingredients starting with water down to the active dry yeast.

Choose the basic bread setting. Select the crust, then the color and then the loaf size.

Start baking by following the manual instructions, and check the dough after five minutes of mixing.

Add in 1 to 2 tablespoons of flour or water if really needed. Add in the olives, when your machine signals that the final kneading is almost finished.

Note: The time-delay feature of this bread machine is not recommended for this recipe.

Enjoy!

Nutritional Information: 124 calories; 4 g fat (2 g saturated fat); 9 mg cholesterol; 299 mg sodium; 19 g carbohydrate; 1 g total sugars; 1 g dietary fiber; 5 g protein.

Stromboli Ladder Loaf

This loaf bread is loaded with pizza filling and baked in your bread machine pan for twenty minutes only after 25 minutes of preparation. The zesty bread complements with the cheesy filling, which makes it an excellent meal for your weeknight dinner.

Servings: 1 loaf (2 pounds)

Ingredients

1 1/2 cups **(70° to 80°) water**

2 tablespoons **canola oil**

1 teaspoon of **lemon juice**

2 tablespoons of **nonfat dry milk powder**

2 tablespoons **white sugar**

1 teaspoon **salt**

4 cups **bread flour**

3 teaspoons **active dry yeast**

Filling:

3/4 cup **pizza sauce**

1 package sliced **pepperoni** (3-1/2 ounces)

2 cups **part-skim mozzarella cheese shredded**

1/2 cup **grated Parmesan cheese**

1 tablespoon **water**

1 large **egg white**

Directions

Place in a bread machine pan the first 8 ingredients in their particular order.

Choose the dough setting. Double check the dough after mixing for 5 minutes and see if it needs an additional 1 to 2 tablespoons water or flour.

Turn the dough on a flour-dusted surface when the cycle is finished.

Roll the dough into a 15by12-inch rectangle; place on a buttered baking sheet.

Spread the pizza sauce in a three-inch wide long strip down the middle part of the dough to traverse within two inches of its ends.

Neatly arrange the pepperoni on top of long strips of pizza sauce and top it with Parmesan and mozzarella cheeses.

Cut one-inch wide strips on the long side of pizza sauce, about 2 ½ inches into the middle part. Fold beginning at one end of the strips and fold the alternating pizza strips at an angle across the filling. To seal, pinch the end tightly.

To make the egg wash, beat the egg white in water and brush over the dough.

Bake for twenty to twenty-five minutes at 425 degrees F, until golden brown. Let cool on wire racks for ten minutes and cut into slices.

Note: The time-delay feature of this bread machine is not recommended for this recipe.

Enjoy!

Nutritional Information: 259 calories; 7 g fat (3 g saturated fat); 24 mg cholesterol; 554 mg sodium; 34 g carbohydrate; 4 g total sugars; 1 g dietary fiber; 15 g protein.

CHEESY SAUSAGE LOAF

Whip up a contest winning bread loaf filled with provolone and mozzarella cheeses, garlic powder and sausage for your dinner, breakfast or brunch. It is moist inside and a perfect shiny golden crust. This scrumptious loaf will be ready after 75 minutes.

Servings: 1 loaf (16 slices)

Ingredients

1 cup **(70° to 80°) water**

4 teaspoons softened **butter**

1 1/4 teaspoons **salt**

1 teaspoon **sugar**

3 cups **bread flour**

2 1/4 teaspoons **active dry yeast**

3/4 cup **provolone cheese shredded**

1 pound **cooked and drained bulk pork sausage**

1/4 teaspoon **garlic powder**

3/4 cup **part-skim mozzarella cheese shredded**

Pepper to taste

1 lightly beaten **egg**

Directions

In a bread machine, place the ingredients in this order: water, butter, salt, sugar, flour and active dry yeast.

Choose the dough setting and check it after the ingredients are mixed for five minutes, adding 1 to 2 tablespoons water or flour if the need arises.

Lightly dust your work surface and place the dough when the cycle is completed.

Roll the dough into a 16"by10" rectangle; cover with plastic wrap and let stand in a warm temperature for ten minutes.

Combine in medium-sized bowl the cheeses, pepper, garlic powder and sausage and evenly spread on top of dough within one-half inch of edges.

Roll up to resemble a jelly roll, beginning with the long side and pinch the seam to seal and tuck the ends beneath.

Arrange the roll on an oiled baking sheet with seam side facing down; cover and let stand for thirty minutes until its sized has doubled.

Bake for twenty minutes at 350 degrees F and bake for fifteen to twenty minutes until lightly golden browned. Let cool on wire rack.

Note: The time-delay of your bread machine is not recommended for this recipe.

Serve!

Nutritional Information: 255 calorie; 15.5 g fat (6.4 g saturated fat); 44 mg cholesterol; 636 mg sodium; 18.5 g carbohydrate; 0.8 g dietary fiber; 0.3 g total sugars; 10.5 g protein.

JOHN
MAPLE-GLAZED LONG JOHNS

Have an enjoyable coffee break with these sweet and vanilla-flavored long johns. The gorgeous johns are deep fried and drizzled with maple-cream. They are easy to prepare in 30 minutes and each batch will be ready in five minutes.

Servings: 2-1/2 dozen 3

Ingredients

1 cup **(70° to 80°) water**

1 **egg**

1/2 teaspoon of **vanilla extract**

1/2 cup **sugar**

1/4 cup **shortening**

1/2 teaspoon **salt**

3 cups **bread flour**

2 1/4 teaspoons **active dry yeast**

Oil for **deep-fat frying**

For the glaze:

1 tablespoon **maple flavoring**

1/4 cup **half-and-half cream**

2 cups **confectioners' sugar**

Directions

Place the first eight ingredients in a bread machine pan in their particular order.

Select the dough setting, making sure to check the dough when mixing is finished after five minutes. Add in 1 to 2 tablespoons flour or water if necessary.

Place the dough on a floured work surface once the cycle is completed. Divide the dough into four parts; roll each part into a 12"by5" rectangle. Cut the rectangle crosswise into 1 ½-inch width strips.

Meanwhile, heat the oil in a deep-fat fryer or electric skillet at 375 degrees F. Drop a few strips at a time and cook for 1 minute each side until golden brown. Drain the strips on paper towels. Let cool on a wire rack.

Combine in a small bowl the maple flavoring, half-and-half cream and confectioner's sugar. Drizzle glaze over the long johns.

Note: The time-delay feature of the bread machine is not recommended for this recipe.

Enjoy!

Nutritional Information: 175 calorie; 9.5 g fat (1.7 g saturated fat); 6 mg cholesterol; 45 mg sodium; 21.4 g carbohydrate; 0.4 g dietary fiber; 11.2 g total sugars; 1.6 g protein

BUN

RANCH HAMBURGER BUNS

Get ready with your burger patty and have them filled inside these flavorful, tender and nicely golden buns. Your bread machine pan comes in handy just in case you run out of bun supply. Here you can prepare the buns in 30 minutes and bake in 10 minutes.

Servings: 1 dozen

Ingredients

1/2 cup **(70° to 80°) water**

1/2 cup **plain yogurt**

1 **egg**

3/4 cup **cheddar cheese shredded**

2 tablespoons of **nonfat dry milk powder**

4 1/2 teaspoons **sugar**

1 tablespoon **ranch salad dressing mix**

1 1/2 teaspoons **salt**

3 cups **bread flour**

2 1/4 teaspoons **active dry yeast**

For the egg wash:

2 tablespoons **water**

1 **egg**

Poppy seeds or **sesame seeds** (optional)

Directions

Place in a bread machine pan the first ten ingredients in their particular order.

Opt for the dough setting and don't forget to check the dough right away after it was mixed for 5 minutes. Pour 1 to 2 tablespoons flour or water to the dough if necessary.

Lightly dust a work surface and place the dough on top after the cycle is completed.

Cut the dough into twelve parts and form into round balls.

Coat a jumbo muffin cups with oil and place the dough balls. Cover the pans for forty-five minutes until the size has doubled in a warm place.

Prepare the egg wash by whisking the egg in water and brush over the buns. Sprinkle the buns with sesame or poppy seeds if you wish.

Bake for eight to twelve minutes at 400 degrees F. Remove buns from pan and let cool on wire racks.

Note: The time-delay feature of the bread machine is not recommended for this recipe.

Enjoy!

Nutritional Information: 137 calories; 1 g fat (1 g saturated fat); 20 mg cholesterol; 397 mg sodium; 25 g carbohydrate; 0 g total sugars; 1 g dietary fiber; 7 g protein.

PANETTONE

This Italian sweet bread loaf will make your family proud of you. Each moist slice of this bread is satisfying with its tender texture and the packed with raisins and candied fruit to satisfy your hunger for sweets, done in the convenience of your bread maker.

Servings: 1 loaf (1-1/2 pounds, 10 slices)

Ingredients

2/3 cup **(70° to 80°) water**

1 **egg**

1 teaspoon of **vanilla extract**

1/4 cup softened **butter**

3/4 teaspoon **salt**

2 1/4 cups **bread flour**

2 tablespoons **sugar**

1 tablespoon **nonfat dry milk powder**

1 1/2 teaspoons **active dry yeast**

1/2 cup **golden raisins**

1/2 cup chopped **mixed candied fruit**

Directions

Put together in your bread machine pan the first 9 ingredients starting off with water down to the yeast.

Select the dough setting (bear in mind to check the dough after five minutes of mixing and pour 1 to 2 tablespoons flour or water if the need arises.)

112

When the final kneading is almost finished; add the raisins and candied fruit. Transfer the dough to a lightly dusted floured surface when the cycle is completed.

Shape the dough into a nine-inch round loaf and place on a nine-inch springform pan coated with cooking spray. Cover with plastic wrap; let it rise for forty minutes until its size has doubled.

Bake for twenty-five to thirty minutes at 350 degrees F until golden brown. Let cool on a wire rack and remove the sides of the pan.

Cut the Panettone into wedges.

Serve!

Nutritional Information: 210 calories; 5 g fat (3 g saturated fat); 33 mg cholesterol; 233 mg sodium; 39 g carbohydrate; 16 g total sugars; 2 g dietary fiber; 5 g protein.

BREADSTICKS
HONEY WHEAT BREADSTICKS

These contest winner breadsticks have long shelf life and they are easy to prepare. They are not laborious, and they can be served in 40 minutes. The honey-flavored sticks are ideal for your kid's Bento box and they are not messy.

Servings: 16 breadsticks

Ingredients

1 1/3 cups **(70° to 80°) water**

3 tablespoons of **honey**

2 tablespoons **canola oil**

1 1/2 teaspoons **salt**

2 cups **bread flour**

2 cups **whole wheat flour**

3 teaspoons **active dry yeast**

Directions

Place in a bread machine pan all ingredients in their particular order and then select the dough setting. Check the dough after it has been mixed for five minutes, adding one to two tablespoons water or flour in the need arises.

Once the cycle is completed, transfer the dough to a work surface lightly dusted with flour.

Divide the dough into sixteen portions and form them into individual balls. Roll the balls to form an eight-inch rope.

Arrange the dough ropes on a lightly oiled baking sheets about two inches apart. Cover the sheets with plastic wrap, place in a warm area until the size has doubled for thirty minutes.

Bake for ten to twelve minutes and bake for 375 degrees F until golden brown. Let cool on wire racks.

Note: The time-delay feature of the bread machine is not recommended for this recipe.

Enjoy!

Nutritional Information: 131 calories; 2 g fat (0 saturated fat); 0 mg cholesterol; 222 mg sodium; 25 g carbohydrate; 0 g total sugars; 2 g dietary fiber; 4 g protein.

Soft Italian Breadsticks

Another way to feed your family with delightful snacks is this contest winning breadsticks. It won the hearts of cooking judges because of its soft buttery texture and aromatic flavor. Each oven-fresh breadstick is brushed with butter right away and sprinkled with Parmesan.

Servings: 2 dozens

Ingredients

1 cup **(70° to 80°) water**

3 tablespoons softened **butter**

1 1/2 teaspoons **salt**

3 cups **bread flour**

2 tablespoons **sugar**

1 teaspoon of **Italian seasoning**

1 teaspoon **garlic powder**

2 1/4 teaspoons **active dry yeast**

For the topping:

1 tablespoon melted **butter**

1 tablespoon **Parmesan cheese**, grated

Directions

Place in a bread machine pan all ingredients except the toppings in a particular order as suggested by the manufacturer.

Choose the dough setting, and then check the condition of the dough after mixing for 5 minutes, and decide whether to add 1 to 2 tablespoons of flour or water if the need arises.

Place the dough on a flour-dusted surface when the cycle is completed.

Divide into halve, cutting the halves into twelve parts. Roll each piece into a four-inch to six-inch rope and place on greased baking sheets, at least two inches apart. Cover and let the dough rise for twenty minutes.

Bake for fifteen to eighteen minutes at 350 degrees F until golden brown.

Brush the breadsticks with butter and dust with Parmesan cheese. Serve immediately.

Enjoy!

Nutritional Information: 73 calories; 2 g fat (1 g saturated fat); 5 mg cholesterol; 171 mg sodium; 12 g carbohydrate; 1 g total sugars; 0 g dietary fiber; 2 g protein.

BISCUITS

CRANBERRY BISCUITS

These tender-sweet contest winning biscuits are highly recommended for your brunch, breakfast or get-together. Every bite is a pleasurable experience as you can smell the zest of orange and enjoy its creaminess and buttery texture.

Servings: 1-1/2 dozen

Ingredients

1 2/3 cups **warm (70° to 80°) whole milk**

2 large **eggs**

3 tablespoons softened **butter**

3/4 cup **potato flakes mashed**

1/4 cup **sugar**

2 teaspoons **salt**

1 1/4 teaspoons **ground cinnamon**

1 teaspoon **orange zest**, grated

4 cups **bread flour**

1 tablespoon **active dry yeast**

1 cup **dried cranberries**

For the orange glaze:

2 to 3 tablespoons **orange juice**

1 cup **confectioners' sugar**

3 tablespoons **chopped dried cranberries** (optional)

Directions

In your bread machine pan, put the first ten ingredients according to the manufacturer's suggestion. Choose the dough setting, and check if it needs an additional water or flour. Just add 1 to 2 tablespoons water or flour.

When the final kneading is almost finished, add the dried cranberries.

After the cycle is finished, place the dough on a work surface lightly dusted with flour, and cover to rest for fifteen minutes.

Roll the dough into one-half-inch thick and cut using a 2 ½ -inch biscuit cutter.

Neatly arrange the dough in a lightly oiled 15by10by1-inch baking pan. Cover the dough with a plastic wrap, and let stand for forty minutes to double its size.

Bake for ten to fifteen minutes at 375 degrees F until golden brown.

Prepare the glaze by combining in a small bowl the orange juice and confectioner's sugar. Drizzle the glaze over warm biscuits and sprinkle with chopped cranberries if you like.

Note: The time-delay feature of the bread machine is not recommended for this recipe.

Enjoy!

Nutritional Information: 198 calories; 3 g fat (2 g saturated fat); 32 mg cholesterol; 306 mg sodium; 39 g carbohydrate; 15 g total sugars; 1 g dietary fiber; 6 g protein.

KOLACHES

FRUIT-FILLED KOLACHES

These adorable Kolaches are great for snacking and special events. FYI, people from Central Europe serve this bread at parties and wedding celebrations. The taste is not so sweet, yet they are appealing to sweet tooth, and that's because of the goodness of its pastry filling.

Servings: 2 dozens

Ingredients

1 1/4 cups **warm (70° to 80°) water**

1/2 cup softened **butter**

1 large **egg**

1 large **egg yolk**

1 teaspoon of **lemon juice**

1/3 cup **nonfat dry milk powder**

1/4 cup mashed **potato flakes**

1/4 cup **sugar**

1 teaspoon **salt**

3 3/4 cups plus 3 tablespoons **bread flour**

2 teaspoons **active dry yeast**

1 (12 ounces) can **apricot/raspberry cake and pastry filling**

Extra **butter** for brushing

Directions

Place the first eleven ingredients in your bread machine pan in their particular order.

Press the dough setting, checking after when mixing is completed after 5 minutes. Check if it needs an additional 1 to 2 tablespoons water or flour. Dust your work surface with flour and place the dough once the cycle is completed.

Pat the dough or roll into a rectangle, about 15by10 inches. Cover the dough and let stand for ten minutes.

With a biscuit cutter, cut the dough into twenty-four squares.

Fill the center of individual squares with a heaping teaspoonful of the filling.

Make an overlap of 2 opposite dough corners on top of the pastry filling and pinch to seal.

Arrange the dough about two inches apart on oiled baking sheets. Cover with plastic wrap and let rise for one hour.

Bake for eight to ten minutes at 425 degrees F until lightly browned.

Remove the sheets from oven and brush all over with butter. Remove immediately from pans and let cool on wire racks.

Note: The time-delay feature of your bread machine is not recommended to use for this recipe.

Serve!

Nutritional Information: 154 calories; 4 g fat (2 g saturated fat); 28 mg cholesterol; 160 mg sodium; 26 g carbohydrate; 7 g total sugars; 1 g dietary fiber; 4 g protein.

CRESCENTS

ALMOND CRESCENTS

Crescents baked in your bread machine pan are a great way to please your loved ones, if they've been used to eating the same type of bread every day. Now it's time to prepare these glossy and tender crescents flavored with almond extract and packed with almond, cornmeal, and butter filling.

Servings: 2 dozens

Ingredients

1/2 cup **warm (70° to 80°) whole milk**

2 **eggs**

1/4 cup softened **butter**

1 1/2 teaspoons of **almond extract**

1/3 cup **sugar**

1/2 teaspoon **salt**

3 cups & extra 2 tablespoons **bread flour**

2 1/4 teaspoons **active dry yeast**

For the filling:

1 teaspoon **almond extract**

2 tablespoons melted **butter**

1/2 to 3/4 cup sliced **almonds**

2 tablespoons **cornmeal**

1 tablespoon **water**

1 **egg**

Directions

Place together in a bread machine pan the first 8 ingredients starting with warm whole milk and end in yeast as recommended by the manual instructions.

Choose the dough setting, checking it after five minutes of mixing, and add water or flour (1 to 2 tablespoons) if the need arises.

Transfer the dough on a work surface sprinkled with flour when the cycle is finished; divide into half and roll into a twelve-inch circle.

Now, combine the almond extract and butter and use this to brush the dough. Cut the circles into twelve wedges and sprinkle with almonds. Roll up the wedge starting from its wide end.

Coat the baking sheets with cooking spray, and dust with cornmeal.

Arrange the rolls with pointed side facing down, on the pans, at least two-inches apart. Create a curve on the ends of each roll to resemble a crescent moon. Cover and keep in a warm place to double its size for fifty minutes.

Prepare the egg wash by beating the egg in water and brush on top of dough.

Bake for thirteen to fifteen minutes at 350 degrees F until golden brown. Let cool on wire racks.

Note: The time-delay feature of the bread machine is not recommended for this recipe.

Serve!

Nutritional Information: 118 calories; 5 g fat (2 g saturated fat); 35 mg cholesterol; 89 mg sodium; 16 g carbohydrate; 3 g total sugars;1 g fiber; 4 g protein.

CONGRATULATIONS!

YOU HAVE MADE IT TO THE END ! AS A TOKEN OF OUR APPRECIATION PLEASE CLICK ON THE BOOK BELOW AND ENTER YOUR EMAIL ADDRESS TO SUBSCRIBE TO OUR NEWSLETTER & CLAIM YOUR FREE COOKBOOK!

CONCLUSION

Thank you so much for downloading this eBook. We at Savour Press hope this book has increased your knowledge regarding some unique and healthy bread machine recipes. This eBook contains a curated list of what we believe to be the 45 best bread machine recipes which represent a variety of flavors, tastes, methods, preparation time and baking time. All different categories of bread machine recipes are represented such as bread, twist, bun, focaccia, kolach, Panettone, biscuit, loaf, bagels, rolls, crescents, and many more.

While preparing these recipes, we decided to offer you the best we could, so that you won't have a hard time looking for ingredients by compiling the recipes that are simple and quick to do with ingredients that can be found in the nearby grocery store, and that they are within your budget means. Since you've been finding ways to please your loved ones, and treat them with the best cuisine and dishes, we are sure that they will be proud of your efforts. We hope you will enjoy cooking with these recipes.

Thanks again for your support.

Happy Cooking!

Made in the USA
Middletown, DE
26 March 2021